What's Going to Happen Next?

Kids in the Juvenile Court System

KIDS HAVE *TROUBLES* TOO

What's Going to Happen Next?

Kids in the Juvenile Court System

by Sheila Stewart and Camden Flath

Mason Crest Publishers

MASON CREST PUBLISHERS INC.
370 Reed Road
Broomall, Pennsylvania 19008
(866)MCP-BOOK (toll free)
www.masoncrest.com

First Printing
9 8 7 6 5 4 3 2 1

Library of Congress Cataloging-in-Publication Data

Stewart, Sheila, 1975–
  What's going to happen next? : kids in the juvenile court system / by Sheila Stewart and Camden Flath.
        p. cm.
  Includes bibliographical references and index.
  ISBN (set) 978-1-4222-1691-0   ISBN 978-1-4222-1693-4
  ISBN (ppbk set) 978-1-4222-1904-1   ISBN 978-1-4222-1906-5 (pbk.)
  1. Juvenile courts—United States—Juvenile literature 2. Children—Legal status, laws, etc.—United States—Juvenile literature. I. Flath, Camden, 1987- II. Title.
  KF9795.S74 2010
  345.73'081—dc22
                                                2010017063

Design by MK Bassett-Harvey.
Produced by Harding House Publishing Service, Inc.
www.hardinghousepages.com
Cover design by Torque Advertising + Design.
Printed in USA by Bang Printing.

The creators of this book have made every effort to provide accurate information, but it should not be used as a substitute for the help and services of trained professionals.

Introduction

Each child is unique—and each child encounters a unique set of circumstances in life. Some of these circumstances are more challenging than others, and how a child copes with those challenges will depend in large part on the other resources in her life.

The issues children encounter cover a wide range. Some of these are common to almost all children, including threats to self-esteem, anger management, and learning to identify emotions. Others are more unique to individual families, but problems such as parental unemployment, a death in the family, or divorce and remarriage are common but traumatic events in many children's lives. Still others—like domestic abuse, alcoholism, and the incarceration of a family member—are unfortunately not uncommon in today's world.

Whatever problems a child encounters in life, understanding that he is not alone is a key component to helping him cope. These books, both their fiction and nonfiction elements, allow children to see that other children are in the same situations. The books make excellent tools for triggering conversation in a nonthreatening way. They will also promote understanding and compassion in children who may not be experiencing these issues themselves.

These books offer children important factual information—but perhaps more important, they offer hope.

—*Cindy Croft, M.A., Ed., Director of the Center for Inclusive Child Care*

Jamie lay on the thin hard mattress and wondered how he was supposed to sleep here. Too much had happened that day. Things he didn't want to think about but which kept swirling through his head. He was in jail—well, not jail exactly, but kid-jail, a juvenile detention center. When he'd woken up that morning, this was the last place he'd thought he would be.

He wished he could just fall asleep and wake up in his own bed. This would all be a horrible, terrible dream. He could just go back to his old life. It hadn't been a great life, true, but it was better than being here.

The memories he didn't want to think about ran through his head again: He was late for school, so he'd cut through the alley behind the gas station. He'd seen something move next to the dumpster. It was a rat, but once he'd looked in that direction, he saw something else. A gun lay on the ground, a rag half wrapped around it. He'd picked it up, thought about Mark, and put it in his backpack. Mark was always mean to him, and it had gotten so bad that he didn't even want to go to school anymore. He'd told Dad, but Dad, as usual, just made him feel worse. "Don't be such a wimp, Jamie," he'd said. "If he's messing with you, just mess with him right back. Don't let him push you around."

A gun would scare Mark, he'd thought. Then he would never mess with Jamie again. He would point the gun at Mark, and then Mark would leave him alone.

But he didn't get that far, as it turned out. The girl behind him in class had seen the gun when he opened his backpack, and she'd told the teacher. Then he'd had to go to the principal's office and the principal had called his dad and the police.

So then the police had come and arrested him. Dad had come to the police station and screamed at him. "Barely ten years old and your life is already ruined," Dad had yelled.

And now he was here. "Taking a gun to school is very, very serious," the police detective had told Jamie. "We can't release you without a judge saying it's okay." But no judge was available for a detention hearing until the next afternoon, so Jamie had had to go here, to the juvenile detention center.

He hadn't known taking a gun to school was illegal, although he'd figured his teacher probably wouldn't like it if she found out. He didn't know anything about the law. He didn't know anything about guns, either. He hadn't even known if the gun was loaded, but the police said it was.

Somehow, in the middle of all these thoughts, he finally fell asleep and slipped into a bad dream.

During his whole time at the juvenile detention center, Jamie felt like he must be still dreaming. He still couldn't believe he was actually there. A bell woke him up in the morning. He ate breakfast in the cafeteria with a bunch of other kids and then had to go to a classroom, where a teacher gave them schoolwork. Jamie had trouble focusing on the schoolwork, though, because all he could do was wonder what was going to happen to him next.

At three o'clock in the afternoon, Jamie had to leave for his detention hearing at court. His dad came to the detention center with clean clothes for him to wear, and he brought with him a lawyer to represent Jamie.

At court, the detention hearing turned out to be very short. Jamie almost felt disappointed. He'd spent a night and most of a day in the juvenile detention center, waiting to see the judge, and then the judge had just glanced at the file and said Jamie could go home with his dad. He would come back to court in a month for a jurisdiction hearing and the judge would decide whether or not Jamie had committed a crime.

Jamie didn't know if he really wanted to go home with his dad. Maybe the juvenile detention center would have actually been better.

He followed his dad and the lawyer slowly down the hall, scuffing his feet. He wondered if everyone who saw him could tell he was a criminal.

"Hurry up, Jamie!" Dad snapped. "I want to get out of here. Because of you I've lost two days of work, you know." He turned back and kept talking to the lawyer. He still hadn't introduced the lawyer to Jamie.

In the parking garage, Jamie climbed into the backseat of the car, while his dad said goodbye to the lawyer and then got into the front seat. He looked at Jamie in the mirror.

"Well," he said heavily, "you have really messed up this time. I don't even know what I'm going to do with you. You've been kicked out of school, but I have to make sure you get an education. How am I supposed to work if you're out of school?"

Jamie didn't answer. He didn't know the answers. He just felt overwhelmed and miserable.

By the time of the jurisdictional hearing, some of those answers had been worked out. Jamie was going to an alternative school for the rest of the year. He had been set to go into middle school for the next year anyway, and they had said they'd accept him there unless he caused further trouble. But he didn't plan on doing that.

In some ways, he liked the alternative school better. For one thing, Mark wasn't there. The classes were really small, and the teachers were nice. He hadn't really had any friends at his old school anyway. Not since Sam had moved away last year. He'd expected the kids here to be mean and scary, since they were all here because they'd had trouble in their regular schools. Some of them were a little scary, but they weren't too bad, and there were always teachers around to make sure nobody could get too mean.

On the morning of the hearing, Jamie and his dad drove to a coffee shop to meet with the lawyer. Jamie had finally discovered that the lawyer's name was David Hassan. He was young and seemed to have lots of energy. Jamie liked him, which surprised him. He treated Jamie like a real person and told him to call him by his first name. Jamie didn't think his dad liked him, though. He seemed to have hired him because David didn't cost as much as most lawyers.

"Hey, Jamie," David said. "How's it going? Are you nervous?"

"Of course," Jamie said. "Are you?"

"Show some respect," Dad said, but David laughed.

"I'm not too nervous," he said. "But that's because I'm pretty confident about what's going to happen."

"What's going to happen?" Jamie asked.

"Meg has written up a report that she'll give to the judge and the District Attorney at the disposition hearing," David said. "That report includes her recommendation that you be released to your father's custody and placed on probation for six months. I'm fairly confident the judge will agree with her recommendation."

Meg was the probation officer, but Jamie didn't call her Meg, he called her Ms. Hayworth. She was nice, but a little more serious than David, and Jamie always felt a little nervous around her.

"What's this dispositional hearing?" Jamie's dad asked. "I thought he was having a jurisdictional hearing today?"

"The jurisdictional hearing is first," David said, "but since Jamie isn't contesting the petition, that hearing should be pretty short, and we've scheduled the dispositional hearing for this afternoon. The dispositional hearing is where the judge decides what should happen next. If Jamie was an adult being tried in criminal court, this would be the sentencing portion."

"So it will all be over after today?" Jamie asked. He wondered if he could even hope that was true.

"Not entirely," David said. "You'll still have to follow whatever the judge decides."

"Your actions have consequences," Dad said. "Don't forget that."

By the time they were ushered into the courtroom for the dispositional hearing, Jamie was shaking. The jurisdictional hearing had been very short, just as David had said it would be. All he had had to do was say he really had brought the gun to school. Just saying those words had been hard, though. His voice and his legs had shook and his eyes had filled with tears.

"It's going to be okay, right, Dad?" he asked now, as they waited for the judge to come in.

His dad shook his head. "I don't know, Jamie," he said. "You messed up, and you'll just have to wait and see what the judge says."

David put his hand on Jamie's shoulder. "It is going to be okay," he said in Jamie's ear. "What-ever happens, there are going to be people around

to help you get through this. You already know you made a mistake, but we're making things right."

Jamie watched Judge Sinclair walk into the court and sit down behind her desk. She looked over the papers on her desk and then looked up.

"James Callahan," she said to Jamie. "You have admitted to possession of a concealed weapon, possession of a weapon by a minor, and bringing a gun onto school property. I've read the report from Officer Megan Hayworth. She has noted that this is your first offence, that you have generally done well in school apart from this incident, and that there was a certain amount of ignorance on your part in regards to the crime. Ignorance of the law is not an excuse, but I have taken it into consideration, especially since you are so young."

She looked up at Jamie and he thought he was going to cry again. He didn't understand everything the judge was saying, so he wasn't sure if things were going well or not.

"Therefore," Judge Sinclair continued, "it is my decision that the minor, James Callahan, be released into his father, Scott Callahan's, custody, with the following provisions:

"First, that the minor, James Callahan, be placed on probation for a period of six months, during which his behavior will be monitored by a probation officer.

"And second, that the minor, James Callahan, and his father, Scott Callahan, attend counseling, both separately and together, for the purpose of rehabilitation and to prevent any similar incidents in the future."

And then, suddenly, it was over. The judge left the courtroom and David hugged Jamie.

"See," he said, "I told you it would be okay."

"Was it okay?" Jamie asked. "What just happened?" He felt a little dizzy.

"What was that part about counseling?" his dad asked. "I don't want to get counseling."

"It definitely was okay," David said to Jamie, and then turned to his dad. "Since Judge Sinclair ordered counseling, you will need to do it," he said. "But it will probably be good for you and Jamie anyway."

Jamie's dad looked annoyed, but he didn't argue anymore.

"Things are going to get better, Jamie," David said. "You didn't ruin your life. Take advantage of the counseling to learn what you can. Maybe one day you'll be in court again as a lawyer."

"I don't know about that," Jamie said, but he smiled, thinking about it. He had been dreading for weeks what the judge might say, but now he felt like a big rock had been taken off his chest and he could breathe again. Happiness washed over him and he laughed.

"My life is not ruined!" he said, and threw his arms around his dad.

His dad looked startled for a minute and then awkwardly hugged him back. "No, I guess not," he said. "Looks like you're going to do okay after all."

Jamie laughed again. He felt better than he had in a long time.

Kids in the Juvenile Court System

Jamie broke the law by picking up the gun he found and carrying it to school. After Jamie brings the gun to school, he is arrested by the police and goes into what is called the juvenile court system. Juvenile courts are a separate court system for young people who break the law. When kids are guilty of breaking the law, the set of rules that everyone must follow, the juvenile court system makes sure they don't break the law again.

Understand the Word

Consequences are things that happen because something else happens. If you go outside when it's raining, the consequence will be that you get wet. If you do something wrong, the consequences may be that people are angry with you or you have to do something to pay for what you did.

In court Jamie has a lawyer who argues his side of the story to a judge, the person making decisions about the **consequences** of Jamie's actions. Like Jamie, kids who break the law may have to go to counseling, so that they can talk to an adult about the sort of problems at school that made Jamie think it was okay to take the gun he found.

If kids' crimes are more serious, or they have broken the law many times, they may go to juvenile detention, a sort of jail for kids or teens, for a long period of time.

Most of Jamie's story takes place in a courtroom, which is located inside a courthouse.

Think of the juvenile court system as a process with many steps in it. Each of these parts is important to the system. Judges, lawyers, police, parents, and young people all have roles in the juvenile courts.

Just like Jamie, kids in the juvenile court system have to go through different hearings that help decide what the consequences for their breaking the law will be. In most cases, the juvenile court is working to help kids, not punish them. The court tries its best to think of what will be best for the kid who has broken the law.

Understand the Word

Tried, when it's used the way it is here, means the process of going to court for a crime and eventually receiving a sentence (the consequence the judge decides on).

What Is a Juvenile?

Each state in the country decides when a kid can be **tried** as an adult for crimes they commit. For most states, this age is 18. In these states, after a person is 18 years old, they are treated like an adult under the law. Adults have much more serious consequences for breaking the law, including time in prison. In Georgia, Texas, Illinois, Louisiana, and a few other states, a person is considered an adult after they turn 17. Four states—Connecticut, New York, North Carolina, and Vermont—treat everyone over the age of 16 who breaks the law as an adult. Wyoming is the only state in the country where a person can only be treated as an adult in court after the age of 19.

A juvenile is anyone who cannot be treated as an adult when they commit a crime. If you are under the age that your state has set for when they treat people as adults under the law, you are considered a juvenile. In the United States, 1 out of every 4 people are younger than 18. That's 70 million people who are considered juveniles in most states.

In some cases, juveniles who **commit** crimes that hurt others may be tried as adults. Many states have laws that allow them to treat juveniles as adults if they are above a certain age and commit crimes that are very serious. In Georgia, juveniles who are 14 or older can be tried as adults if they commit a crime that hurts others. In some other states, juveniles 15 or older can be tried as adults for some crimes.

Understand the Word

Commit means to do.

Every State Does Things Differently

In each state, kids and teens who have broken the law are handled differently. Your state's juvenile courts may

This boy would be considered a juvenile in most states. That means he would be tried in juvenile court, rather than being tried as an adult.

be set up in a different way from another state's. All the juvenile court systems in the United States, however, are also the same in many ways. Police officers and judges make many decisions about how to make sure kids who have broken the law understand that what they did was wrong and that they don't do it again. These decisions are mostly the same in each state, even if the court system is different in some ways.

What Happens When a Kid Breaks the Law?

If a kid breaks the law and is arrested, police officers have a few choices of what to do next.

Police usually talk with the kid who has broken the law, their parents, and anyone who was hurt by the juvenile's crime. The police officer will also check to see if the kid who broke the law has been in the juvenile court system before. The officer then has to decide to send the kid's case to the juvenile court system or let the kid go with a warning not to get in trouble again. The police can also decide to send the kid and her parents to see another officer at a juvenile center (like the one Jamie went to) at a later time, if they think the crime isn't serious enough to send the kid to court. Police can also decide to let someone go at the time he is arrested, at the police station, or at the juvenile center.

In 2005, just under 1 in 5 kids was let go with a warning by police who arrested them. Most kids, though—70 percent of all juveniles arrested—were sent to the juvenile court system.

What Kinds of Crimes Are Kids Arrested For?

When Jamie brings the gun to school, he's breaking the law. What Jamie did would get an adult in trouble with the law. If a kid commits a crime that would get an adult arrested and sent to court, he can end up in juvenile court. The sort of crimes that would get an adult arrested are called delinquent acts when juveniles commit them. Delinquent acts include many different crimes. Here are a few examples of delinquent acts that juveniles are arrested for:

- Burglary: Burglary means breaking into a house or other building. It can also mean breaking into someone else's car. If someone goes into a house that is not his, planning to steal something, that is burglary. In 2005, 97,600 burglary cases were tried in juvenile court.

- Robbery: Robbery means taking someone else's things from them. In 2005, 26,000 robbery cases were tried in juvenile court.
- Car theft: The word "theft" means stealing. A juvenile can be arrested for car theft if they try and take someone else's car. In 2005, juvenile courts tried 32,900 car theft cases.
- Weapons **offenses**: A weapons offense means carrying, selling, or using a dangerous weapon. In 2005, 43,600 weapons offense cases were handled by juvenile courts.

> ### *Understand the Word*
> An **offense** is something bad that's done.

In many states, some crimes can be committed only by juveniles. Many laws only cover young people. Breaking those laws does not always come with the same consequences as other crimes. In many cases, kids who break these laws are not considered to have committed a crime at all. Often, the term "status offense," rather than a delinquent act, is used to talk about breaking laws that only apply to young people.

Here are a few examples of status offenses:

- Underage drinking: The drinking age is 21 years old. Anyone under 21 who drinks or carries alcohol is breaking the law.
- Running away: Running away from home without coming back or telling your parents is against the law in many places.
- Skipping school: It is the law that all kids must go to school. If you skip school, you are breaking the law.

What Happens After a Kid Is Arrested?

After Jamie is arrested at school, he has to stay in a juvenile detention center. Kids who are arrested, but have not gone through juvenile court yet, may be held at a juvenile detention center like the one where Jamie goes. While their case is being worked out, juvenile courts may keep kids who have broken the law in a juvenile detention center. If the court believes that kids who have broken the law should be

Underage drinking is illegal, and could get you arrested if the police catch you.

kept away from others, they can be kept at a juvenile detention center.

Once a juvenile's case is sent to the court system, and the kid who broke the law is at a detention center, people in the court system must decide if the case should move forward or the kid should be let go with a warning. A person called a **probation** officer can decide if a crime is serious enough for the kid who broke the law to be sent to court. The probation officer can let the kid go with a warning at this point. She can also put the kid on what is called "informal probation," where the officer and parents of a kid who broke the law decide what would be the best way to make sure she doesn't do it again. This might mean going to counseling, doing something in the community that helps other, or staying in school, for example. Informal probation usually lasts six months. This kind of treatment is usually only for kids who tell the truth about breaking the law and promise not to do it again.

If a probation officer thinks that a kid's crime is serious enough to move forward, he may file what is called a "petition" with the court. Filing a petition

Understand the Word

Probation is a period of time during which the court will keep track of a person and make sure she doesn't get in trouble again.

means that the probation officer is telling the court that the juvenile broke the law, and that the court should decide what consequences are in line with the juvenile's crime. If a kid doesn't follow the rules of her informal probation, her probation officer may file a petition and send her case to juvenile court, as well. In some very serious cases, a probation officer may tell the court that a juvenile's case should be handled as an adult case.

In some courts probation officers work with prosecutors to make decisions about which cases to send to juvenile court. Prosecutors are lawyers who work for the state. Their job is to make sure that if a juvenile breaks the law, the consequences are in line with their crime.

> ### *Understand the Word*
>
> A **hearing** is a meeting in a courtroom, where the judge listens to what the accused person and his lawyers have to say.

What Is a Detention Hearing?

A detention **hearing** must be held within 24 hours of a juvenile being sent to a juvenile detention center. This amount of time is the same for every state in the country. At a detention hearing, a judge looks over everything to do with a juvenile's case and decides if it is

A judge oversees a courtroom hearing, and will decide whether a kid stays in a juvenile detention center.

best to keep her at a juvenile detention center. If a kid is already being held at a juvenile detention center, the judge will decide whether or not to keep the kid in the detention center. Judges can also decide that keeping a kid in a juvenile detention center isn't what is best for her. In this case, the judge can send a juvenile who has broken the law home with her parents. In Jamie's detention hearing, he was sent home with his dad, for example.

In all hearings in the juvenile court system, kids and their parents have lawyers helping them argue their sides of the story. Lawyers who understand everything about the law and court system are experts in making sure that kids are treated fairly and have their side of things heard.

What Is a Jurisdictional Hearing?

A jurisdictional hearing is set up after a detention hearing. In some cases, a jurisdictional hearing will be the first hearing in a juvenile's case. Jurisdictional hearings are called adjudicatory hearings in some states.

At a jurisdictional hearing, a judge decides whether or not the petition filed by the probation officer and/ or prosecutors is true. This means they are deciding whether or not the juvenile committed the crime. The judge starts by reading the petition to the juvenile, his parents, and his lawyer. The judge will ask the juvenile if he did do what the petition says he did. At this point, the kid can say that it is true, that he did break the law, or that he did not. If he says he did not break the law or do what the petition says he did, his lawyer has to argue that the kid is telling the truth. In Jamie's case, the judge asked him if he really did bring the gun to school and he said that he did.

The judge then decides if the petition that says how the kid broke the law is true. If he decides that the petition is true, another hearing—called a disposition hearing—is set up to decide how to treat and care for the kid who broke the law. If the judge decides that the petition isn't true, that the kid did not break the law the way the petition says she did, the judge will let the juvenile go home. When this happens, the juvenile's case is said to be dismissed.

What Is a Disposition Hearing?

A disposition hearing is the final decision in a juvenile court case. The word "disposition" in this case means decision.

Before a disposition hearing takes place, a team of probation officers look at the juvenile's case. They must come up with a disposition plan for the kid who has broken the law. The plan must be focused on what the juvenile's needs are. Probation officers may order that kids go through medical tests and talk with adults about themselves. The officers' plan will be given to the judge at the disposition hearing, and it may be-

If you have been arrested, you might end up in a courtroom like this one. Disposition hearings often happen in these sorts of courtrooms.

come part of his final decision on what to do with a juvenile's case.

In a disposition hearing, the judge decides what is the best thing for the juvenile who broke the law. Prosecutors and juveniles themselves can talk to the judge about different ideas as to what to do with a juvenile's case. After hearing these arguments, and

Formal probation can include counseling, either for yourself or for your family. Counseling isn't anything to be scared of; in the long run, it will help you sort out your problems.

thinking over each choice carefully, judges decide how to best make sure that kids who have broken the law:

- don't do it again.
- understand that they are responsible for their actions.
- get help from adults if they need it, so that they are better off because of the court, not worse.

Judges must also make sure they are thinking of how to keep their community safe, as well as how to make sure anyone hurt by a juvenile's crime are taken care of.

What Happens After a Disposition Hearing?

After many hearings and many decisions made by different people, the judge's disposition is the final word on what is going to happen to a kid who broke the law.

One of the more common decisions judges make is to put kids who have broken the law on formal probation. Jamie is put on probation at the end of his disposition hearing, for instance. Like informal probation, formal probation may include counseling, as it does for Jamie and his dad; community service; or a weekend in a juvenile detention center. A kid's probation may last for a long time, without any end date set, or it may be for only a few months. If a kid on probation follows the rules the judge has set up, the judge will end her case, and she'll be finished with the court system. In 2005, 3 out of 5 juveniles in disposition hearings were placed on formal probation.

The judge may decide that the juvenile who broke the law must go to live in a juvenile residential facility,

Judges often send juvenile criminals to residential facilities, which may be similar to adult jails, like this one. In other cases, residential facilities are more homelike.

away from his parents and home. "Residential facility" just means a place to live. This place can be either very much like a prison or jail, where kids must follow many rules and stay for a long time, or it can be more like a real home. In some states, judges decide to send the juvenile to the state's corrections department, which will make the choice of where the juvenile should be sent and when he can get out. In other cases, judges make the decision of where to send kids who have broken the law. Hearings are held over time to make sure that the kid who broke the law is doing better.

Remember, the juvenile court system isn't just there to punish kids who get into trouble with the law. It is also there to help kids get back on track when they make mistakes. The juvenile court system tries its best to think about what is best for the kid who has broken the law. The court makes its decisions with the community and the juvenile in mind. Just as Jamie is sent to counseling with his dad, other kids in the juvenile court system get help, as well. Jamie's case is just one example of the thousands of cases that go through the juvenile court system each year.

Questions to Think About

1. Do you like Jamie's father? Why or why not? Why do you think he acts the way he does? What do you think he's feeling?

2. Do you think it was fair that Jamie got in so much trouble? Why or why not?

3. What do you think will happen next in Jamie's life? Do you think he'll get in such bad trouble again? Why or why not?

4. How do you feel about David? Why?

Further Reading

Barr, Roger. *Overview Series—Juvenile Crime.* Farmington Hills, Mich.: Lucent Books, 2007.

Bianchi, Anne. *Everything You Need to Know About Family Court.* New York: Rosen Publishing, 2009.

Kelly, Zachary A. *Our Court System.* Vero Beach, Fla.: Rourke Publishing, 2009.

Merino, Noel. *Juvenile Crime.* Farmington Hills, Mich.: Greenhaven Press, 2010.

Lange, Donna. *On the Edge of Disaster: Youth in the Juvenile Court System.* Philadelphia, Penn.: Mason Crest Publishers, 2007.

Find Out More on the Internet

Building Blocks for Youth
www.buildingblocksforyouth.org

Inside the Courtroom
www.justice.gov/usao/eousa/kidspage/index.html

International Child and Youth Care Network
www.cyc-net.org

National Center for Juvenile Justice
www.ncjj.org

National Council of Juvenile and Family Court Judges
www.ncjfcj.org

National Youth Court Center
www.youthcourt.net

U.S. Department of Justice, Office of Juvenile Justice
and Delinquency Prevention
www.ojjdp.ncjrs.gov

The websites listed on this page were active at the time of publication. The publisher is not responsible for websites that have changed their address or discontinued operation since the date of publication. The publisher will review and update the websites upon each reprint.

Index

Picture Credits

Booth, Adam; fotolia: p. 42
Burkard, Sascha; fotolia: p. 28
GOL; fotolia: p. 25
Junial Enterprises; fotolia: p. 36

Karuka; fotolia: p. 33
Martinez, Geo; fotolia: p. 39
Young, Lisa F.; fotolia: p. 40

To the best knowledge of the publisher, all images not specifically credited are in the public domain. If any image has been inadvertently uncredited, please notify Harding House Publishing Service, 220 Front Street, Vestal, New York 13850, so that credit can be given in future printings.

About the Authors

Sheila Stewart has written several dozen books for young people, both fiction and nonfiction, although she especially enjoys writing fiction. She has a master's degree in English and now works as a writer and editor. She lives with her two children in a house overflowing with books, in the Southern Tier of New York State.

Camden Flath is a writer living and working in Binghamton, New York. He has a degree in English and has written several books for young people. He is interested in current political, social, and economic issues and applies those interests to his writing.

About the Consultant

Cindy Croft, M.A. Ed., is Director of the Center for Inclusive Child Care, a state-funded program with support from the McKnight Foundation, that creates, promotes, and supports pathways to successful inclusive care for all children. Its goal is inclusion and retention of children with disabilities and behavioral challenges in community child care settings. Cindy Croft is also on the faculty at Concordia University, where she teaches courses on young children with special needs and the emotional growth of young children. She is the author of several books, including *The Six Keys: Strategies for Promoting Children's Mental Health*.

240825434